EXCALIBUR

RETOLD & ILLUSTRATED BY

CAROL HEYER

Ideals Children's Books ✠ *Nashville, Tennessee*

Published by Ideals Publishing Corporation
Nashville, Tennessee 37210

Printed and bound in the United States of America.

Library of Congress Cataloging-in-Publication Data

Heyer, Carol, 1950-
Excalibur/retold and illustrated by Carol Heyer.
p.   cm.
Summary: King Arthur loses his sword in battle with
the Black Knight and receives a new one, Excalibur,
from the Lady of the Lake.
ISBN 0-8249-8487-0
1. Arthurian romances. [1. Arthur, King. 2. Knights
and knighthood—Folklore. 3. Folklore—England.]
I. Title.
PZ8.1.H487Ex   1991
398.2—dc20   91-9100
                                    CIP
                                    AC

For my parents, Merlyn and Bill, and also for Suzan,
who are always there for me with their help and
support.

A thank-you to the models that posed for this book:
Sage San Martin ....King Arthur
Jay Marr ....Merlin
Greg Bond ....the Black Knight
Sandra Roberts ....the Lady of the Lake
Souhil Rezghi..Bedivere
Carl Bramblett..the herald
Nicholas Guarino..the page

- C.H.

The illustrations in this book were rendered in
pencils and acrylics using live models.
The text type was set in Trump Mediæval.
The display type was set in Lombardic and Delphian.
Color separations were made by Rayson Films, Inc.,
Waukesha, Wisconsin.
Printed and bound by Arcata Graphics Kingsport,
Kingsport, Tennessee.

Designed by Joy Chu.
Consultant: Mary Flowers Braswell.

Long, long ago,

when many kings battled for the throne of England, there was a sword embedded in an enchanted anvil and stone. In golden letters upon the stone was written:

WHOSOEVER PULLETH OUT THIS SWORD

FROM THIS STONE AND ANVIL

IS KING OF ALL ENGLAND

BY RIGHT OF BIRTH.

Many tried and failed to pull the sword from the stone. A day came when young Arthur, not knowing that he was the son of King Uther Pendragon, removed it easily and claimed it for his own.

The people knelt before him, proclaiming him their liege lord. With this same sword, he was dubbed knight and soon after was crowned king.

Arthur chose the bravest and most chivalrous of knights to serve him, and the powerful magician Merlin was his teacher and protector . . .

ONE AFTERNOON, ARTHUR, MERLIN, AND THE KNIGHTS

were at court when the herald sounded the arrival of a visitor. A wounded knight rode into the hall of the great castle Caerleon.

He told of a Black Knight who had set up his pavilion beside the river, at the edge of Camelot. There he challenged every knight who rode past.

Arthur called for his sword, his armor, and his horse. He gathered his best knights and set out to stop the intruder and make the entrance to Camelot safe.

Accompanied by the wizard Merlin, Arthur and his men raced to meet the Black Knight and his company at the river road.

When they neared the pavilion, Arthur saw the challenger's shield leaning against a tree. He reached out his spear, struck the shield, and knocked it to the ground. When the Black Knight heard the clatter, he and his men stomped out of their tent.

"Why do you defy me, sir?" demanded the Black Knight.

"You wounded my knight," Arthur answered. "Those who travel this road are in my domain and under my protection, and you have no right to challenge those who only wish to pass."

Arthur watched the powerful knight pick up his shield and sword. The many men from both sides gathered their weapons, mounted their horses, and readied themselves for war.

The battle began as the two leaders rode toward one another with jousting spears aimed. When they finally clashed, their lances splintered and both men jumped to the ground, drawing their swords.

Equally matched, they fought at close quarters for some time. But the dark knight struck a mighty blow which broke Arthur's weapon in half, destroying the sword from the stone.

Arthur still lunged at the Black Knight with only his shield and broken sword. But the king soon fell to the evil knight's mercy, and the Black Knight knocked him to the ground, raising his weapon to kill.

Arthur's knights fought for their own lives, and none could see him fall. But Merlin was watching the king's battle, and he stepped forward, speaking a spell of enchantment. The Black Knight's sword fell from his hand, the weapons of his followers' dropped to the ground, and they all fell into a deep, magical sleep.

Arthur left his knights on the battlefield and rode quickly away. Angry and ashamed, he had been defeated. He knew that without Merlin's magic, he would be dead. He rode faster and deeper into the forest with Merlin following close behind.

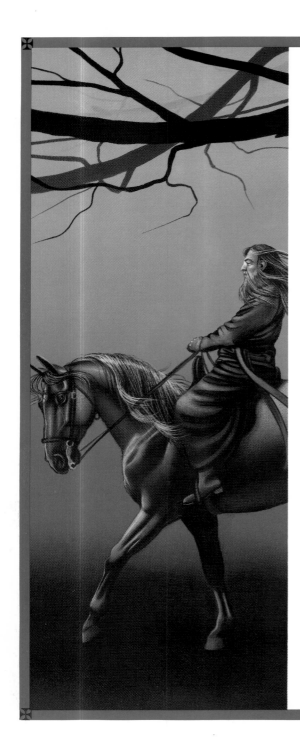

After a time Merlin caught up with Arthur and the two raced side by side. The young king shouted, "I have been defeated and now I am a knight without a sword. I am nothing!"

"There is more to a knight than a sword," Merlin answered, "just as there is more to a king than a crown. You were the bravest of knights when, without a sword, you continued to fight the Black Knight."

"But I lost the battle!" Arthur yelled.

"Arthur, some people let defeat ruin them. Others let victory ruin them. A true knight triumphs equally whether in victory or defeat."

The horses slowed as the two rode deeper into the woods in silence.

"Merlin," Arthur finally said, "I still feel as though I am nothing."

"A battle," Merlin explained, "is merely a contest, something either to win or lose. Neither the win nor the loss makes you triumphant, Arthur. It is only your feelings about yourself which give you triumph or defeat."

As they rode along, Arthur's thoughts returned to his broken sword. As though the wizard knew these thoughts, Merlin spoke again.

"If a sword is all you wish, then I must tell you of a sword of great power and wonder, a sword of kings that might be yours."

"Where can I find this sword?" Arthur asked excitedly.

"Follow me and I will take you to the mystical kingdom of the Lady of the Lake, and to her sword Excalibur, the mightiest of all swords."

Merlin led Arthur to the shore of a great sapphire-blue lake. A thick forest encircled the lake, and water softly lapped against the shore.

"Where is the great kingdom of the lake?" Arthur asked. "And the sword that is to be mine?"

"It is here, before you," Merlin said.

Arthur looked at the forest and wildflowers, the deer and songbird, but could see no castle, no kingdom, no great lady—only sparkling water. Arthur raised his eyebrows and stared at Merlin.

Merlin smiled and said, "Her dominion lies beneath the surface of the water. A magnificent palace and an enchanted faerie realm, as fair as the richest kingdom on earth—this is the lady's kingdom."

The old wizard waved his hand in a circle above the water, and for a moment, the watery depths became like glass.

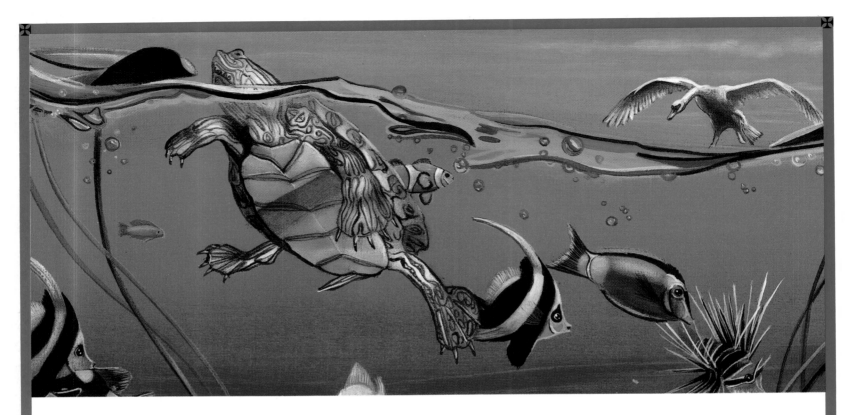

"The lady is a creature of amazing magic," Merlin explained. "The sword she guards is of pure magic, and it is hers alone to give. She will entrust it only to one she finds worthy."

"How shall I obtain the sword if I cannot enter her world?" Arthur asked the wizard.

"If you are chivalrous and ask her kindly, she will come to you," Merlin replied. Arthur stepped to the edge of the lake and touched the water with his hand.

"Lady, please, I wish to speak with you," he said.

Suddenly, the water at the center of the lake began to bubble and swirl. Arthur and Merlin watched a beautiful woman rise from the water and walk over the surface of the lake toward them.

She stopped in front of the king and asked, "What do you seek?"

Arthur answered, "Lady, I have lost my sword in battle and I hope to be found worthy of your sword, Excalibur."

"I know that you are a great king, one that will be remembered for all time," she said softly. "You deserve my sword and I will give it to you. But in return, you must make a promise."

"Anything that you want will be yours," said the king.

The lady answered, "When your days are over, Excalibur must be returned. It must come back to the Lady of the Lake."

"You have my word," he promised.

The woman raised her arm and pointed to the glassy water—again it began to churn. Arthur watched a magnificently sheathed sword pierce through the surface. A woman's hand and arm, sleeved in rich, white silk, held the weapon above the lake.

The sword stood firmly in place until the water became mirror-still. An empty boat appeared, slowly sailing out of the mist. When the vessel reached the shoreline, it stopped in front of Arthur and Merlin, and they both stepped inside. The boat glided to the hand and stopped in front of it. Arthur kneeled, carefully taking Excalibur for himself. Then the empty hand disappeared beneath the water.

Arthur studied the gold scabbard that protected the sword, then taking the sword out of its covering, he held it triumphantly over his head. Excalibur glowed and sparkled, shimmering in a spellbinding brilliance that flowed from the sword and into Arthur. At once he felt the power of the sword, and drawing the weapon before him, he knew that he was honored, indeed, to receive it.

Arthur called out to the Lady of the Lake, "I thank you, fair lady, for this great and wondrous gift."

The Lady of the Lake smiled and nodded. Then she slowly began to sink below the inky water, returning to her own world. The boat returned Merlin and Arthur to land. As they stepped out, remounted their horses, and set off for Camelot, Arthur could think only of Excalibur.

Nearing their kingdom, Merlin asked Arthur, "Which do you think is more powerful, the sword or the scabbard?"

"Without doubt, the sword is the power," said Arthur.

"No, the scabbard is ten times stronger," answered Merlin. "The scabbard's magic is so powerful that no matter how deeply you are wounded in battle, you will not die."

Arthur imagined how he would feel going into battle, knowing that he could not be killed. He had felt the power of Excalibur and wondered if he would be able to use the sword wisely.

The horses' hooves pounded along the path, and Arthur also began to wonder what Merlin meant when he said, "There is more to a knight than a sword."

Beside the path they saw a beautiful tent, and Arthur asked Merlin about it.

"How quickly you have forgotten, child," Merlin answered. "This is the Black Knight's pavilion." They slowed their horses.

"Now that I have a sword, I will defeat him," Arthur whispered to Merlin, drawing Excalibur from its sheath.

"What victory would that be?" Merlin whispered back. "He is weary from fighting. What honor would there be for you to defeat him now?"

Arthur closed his eyes for a moment. He felt the truth in the words of the wise old wizard.

At last, he understood that the outcome of a contest means little. Those who come to know their honor find triumph in each battle, no matter how it ends.

Arthur could feel a deep strength flowing into his heart, and Merlin's words echoed in his mind, "There is more to a knight than a sword." Their horses stopped and Arthur saw the Black Knight coming from the tent, smiling at the young king.

"Black Knight!" Arthur called. "Do you still challenge those who wish to pass?"

"Nay, my lord," the knight answered. "We were somehow enchanted during our battle with you. We awoke to find ourselves surrounded by your good knights, who then spared our lives.

"I shall no longer challenge your domain, and I offer you and your kingdom my services as a knight."

Approaching hoofbeats sounded as the knight knelt before the king, and the company was soon joined by Arthur's trusted knight Bedivere. Without another word, the dark knight, his men, and Bedivere fell in behind Arthur and Merlin and followed them back to Caerleon.

Arthur led the group into the great hall of Caerleon. His knights gathered close by, welcoming the new members of their ranks and congratulating one another for a battle ended in peace.

The sounds of mirth and joy echoed in the many voices, and laughter rang out across the courtyards.

A great feast was prepared, and merriment filled the halls of Caerleon as food and drink were shared in friendship and in tribute to the king.

Arthur's knights listened proudly to their king's story of his quest for the mighty Excalibur, admiring in amazement the beauty of the sword and its magical scabbard.

WITH THE POWER

of Excalibur, the magic of Merlin, and the fellowship of his knights, Arthur ruled over the people of Camelot with wisdom and majesty for many wonderful years.

Arthur became so strong of heart that his reign, his knights, and his kingdom have been remembered long. When Arthur's days came to an end, Excalibur was, indeed, thrown by Bedivere into the lake from which it came . . .

> *AND THERE CAME AN ARM*
>
> *AND A HAND ABOVE THE WATER*
>
> *AND MET IT AND CAUGHT IT,*
>
> *AND SHOOK IT THRICE AND BRANDISHED;*
>
> *AND THEN VANISHED AWAY THE HAND*
>
> *WITH THE SWORD INTO THE WATER.*

- Sir Thomas Mallory
Le Morte D'Arthur